# Key to IP: Identifying Your Patents, Trademarks, Copyrights, and Trade Secrets

CHRIS WEISS

ISBN: 1542813956
ISBN-13: 978-1542813952

# DEDICATION

This book is dedicated to Thea Green, who loves and supports me, and has helped to correct many, many, many mistakes that would have otherwise made it into this book.

# CONTENTS

# DISCLAIMER

This book and all related content is offered for entertainment purposes only and is not intended to serve as legal advice. Any information is provided "as is" without any representations or warranties, express or implied. Complex topics have been simplified for the purposes of explanation. You should contact an attorney for legal advice as specific legal issues cannot be uniformly and accurately addressed.

# 1
# INTRODUCTION

You're at a networking event. Or is it a mixer? A dull murmur fills the air as attendees break off into self-imposed circles of three to five.

You approach one of these circles just in time to hear a man describe his business as "the Uber of dog poop cleanup." "What a coincidence," says the woman to his left, "my business is the Uber of kite flying." They both turn to a third man, who, sensing it is his turn to talk, waves his drink through the air in a dismissive gesture.

"I just help navigate OSHA rules and regulations to ensure a safe working environment for fast-growing companies." The other two members of this impromptu group meet him with blank stares, so he switches to a familiar format. "It's sort of … the Uber of OSHA compliance." They feign a sense of understanding and their talk resumes.

You, meanwhile, keep walking past this minefield of a

conversation in pursuit of the glazed chicken skewers you spied a waiter setting down on a folding table across the room. You prepare a small plate and resolve to talk to the next person you meet.

"So, what brings you here?" you say. "Got a great Uber of something idea?" The confused look you get in response informs you that not everyone has experienced this one-person inside joke. "I'm actually here to network," you say along with your name. You extend your hand.

"My name is Chris Weiss," I say. "Good handshake."

"What brings you here?" you ask.

"Oh, I'm also here to network," I say.

"What do you … What does your company do?"

You expect another answer in a familiar format.

"I'm actually a patent attorney. I help people with intellectual property. Patents, trademarks, copyrights, trade secrets. That sort of thing."

You think about this for a moment. "I've heard patents are bad," you mention. "Don't they stifle innovation?"

"On the contrary. Did you know that the standard of living remained virtually constant for over 1700 years? A person living in the 1700s was not much better off than a person living in 1 AD."

"Huh," you add. "I didn't know that."

"It's true. What finally caused a change was the creation of the first nationwide patent systems. Systems that would reward people for their efforts. Think of how many great ideas there are in this room –"

You scan the room as you recall the conversation you avoided earlier.

"They're not all great …"

"Still, there would be no reason to pursue the promising ideas if someone else could come along and steal them. Having a system of intellectual property creates a reward. It allows investors to connect with smart people so they can both prosper. In exchange, they have to share their idea with the world. Explain how it works."

You think about this.

"Don't get me wrong," I say. "There are definitely abuses, as with any system, but you can't deny the impact on the quality of life. Having a computer in your very pocket –"

I hold up an iPhone® as if it's a wand and I'm either a magician or a conductor.

"This is only possible because of intellectual property. We went from keeping great ideas a secret for a very long time to only recently sharing them with the world. That allows people to build off of the ideas of others."

"Huh," you ponder. "Do you have a business card or something?"

"Even better," I say. I pull a business card out of my wallet and pass it over to you. You turn the card in your hands, feeling a unique texture.

"Oh, this is one of those, what do you call it?" You search for the words. "One of those cards with plant seeds? The kind you can put in the dirt, and it'll grow flowers."

"That's true, but it's so much more. That card in your hands holds an example of each of the main types of intellectual property. Patents, trademarks, copyrights, and trade secrets."

"That's interesting," you note. "I've wanted to learn more about this stuff, but it always feels so overwhelming, kind of like –"

"Networking," I say.

"Yea, kind of like that. I'd love to learn more about this. I mean, I feel like my business could utilize some of these things, but I don't have that much time to sit down and learn it all. In fact, I'm not even sure where to start."

"Why don't I explain it to you right now?" I say. "Using this business card as an example, you can follow along and identify your own intellectual property."

You think about it. About your friend that sold a company for some staggering sum of money because he owned essential patents. About that episode of Shark Tank where Mark Cuban turned down what seemed like a promising company because they didn't have any intellectual property to protect their product.

"Yea, let's do it. Help me identify my intellectual property," you decide. "Just one request."

"Sure, name it," I say.

"Can we get out of this second person tense? It's a good opening, but it'll be awkward to go through all these examples this way."

"Not a problem at all," said Chris Weiss. "Let's begin with patents."

# 2
# UTILITY PATENTS

**Overview**

Most people think of patents as a single thing. In truth, there are three types of patents: utility patents, design patents, and plant patents.

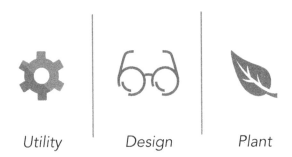

Utility          Design          Plant

The first type of patent is a utility patent. When people say they want to get a patent, they are generally talking about a utility patent. A utility patent protects the useful parts of an invention.

Utility patents can be granted to anyone who invents or discovers any new and useful process, machine, article of manufacture, or composition of matter. It can also be granted to anyone who invents or discovers any new and useful improvement on one of those things. If it's useful, it's a utility patent.

### Stop It!

A lot of people think that patents give you the right to make a product. This isn't true. In fact, it's the complete opposite.

Patents offer the right to *exclude* others from making, using, importing, selling, or offering an invention for sale over a fixed period of time. Basically, patents give you the right to keep others from doing something.

### Filing Deadlines

Ideally, you should never disclose your invention to others until you have a patent application on file. Certain acts, such as publishing a document that details your invention or even offering your invention for sale can prevent you from ever getting a patent on that invention. Even if you fall into an exception for the United States, some of these acts can keep you from ever getting a patent in many foreign countries.

Let's say Mark has a great idea for a smartphone app. He spends his nights and weekends designing this app but doesn't tell anyone about what he's doing. Once it's ready, he publishes a website describing his app and sells it for $0.99. Mark might think he could always patent his app later if sales pick up. The reality is that he likely can't get a patent in the US or any foreign country because of his actions.

Additionally, the United States has adopted a first-to-file patent system, which is in-line with most of the world. This means that the first person to file a patent application on an invention gets that patent. Letting others know about your invention may give your competitors a jumpstart to work on improvements or design-arounds to your invention.

These rules mostly relate to public disclosures, but they also have implications for private disclosures. If you are showing an invention to potential investors, you would ideally have them sign a non-disclosure agreement (NDA) before telling them about your idea. However, many investors, especially angel investors or venture capital funds, will refuse to sign NDAs due to their bargaining position. The only way to actually protect your idea before a pitch is with a patent.

So, to be safe, it is recommended that you never disclose, sell, or offer to sell your invention until you have a patent application filed.

### Filing Process
Application > Examination > Issuance

A utility patent starts life off as a nonprovisional patent application (NPA) containing information about the invention to be protected. This NPA is filed with the United States Patent and Trademark Office, or USPTO for short.

The NPA waits in a queue until an Examiner reviews it at the USPTO. The length of the delay depends on the type of invention as some fields have shorter queues than others. The Examiner will determine whether the NPA is patentable. If the Examiner determines that the NPA isn't patentable, the Examiner will issue an Office action, which is a rejection of one or more components of the application. The inventor, with the help of a patent attorney, can respond to this Office action with a combination of arguments and amendments. A successful response can get an application allowed and issued as a patent.

If the Examiner determines that the NPA is patentable, he or she will issue a Notice of Allowance. The NPA is now ready to issue as a utility patent once some final fees are paid.

### Novelty and Non-obviousness

When an Examiner is determining whether something is patentable, he or she is primarily determining whether the invention is novel and non-obvious. Novel means that no one else has done the same thing as the invention. If you file an NPA on a hammer, and a hammer already exists (it does!), then your NPA application will be rejected for novelty reasons.

Non-obvious means that a combination of known inventions can't be combined to create the invention. If you file an NPA on a hammer with an eraser on the end of it for erasing pencil marks for nail holes, and both a hammer and an eraser already exist (they do!), then your NPA application will be rejected for obviousness reasons.

*Not novel*          *Not non-obvious*

Obviousness rejections can get a lot more complicated in practice, but the basic idea is combining known inventions or elements in an obvious way.

### Utility Patent Lifespan

Your utility patent will last for twenty years from your initial filing date. Note that this date isn't calculated from when your utility patent issues, but from when you first filed an application for your invention.

What if it takes nineteen years from your filing date to get an issued utility patent? Would you only have one year of utility patent coverage? In cases where it takes an exceptionally long time to process your application (i.e., most cases), the USPTO will give you some extra time. This additional time is called "patent term adjustment" and extends the lifetime of a utility patent beyond the twenty-year period from initial filing.

Twenty years, plus whatever bonus time, only applies if you pay maintenance fees throughout the life of your utility patent. Maintenance fees are due at 3.5 years, 7.5 years, and 11.5 years after issuance of your utility patent. By the time these maintenance fees come due, you should have a better understanding of whether this added cost is worth the continued patent protection.

### Utility Patent Claims

There are many elements to an NPA, but the most important, in my opinion, are the claims. Claims determine the scope of patent protection. You get a limited monopoly to keep the public from making and using your invention *as defined by the claims.*

The claims state what you regard as the invention. You only get protection for what you claim. If you claim the right things, you can exclude your competitors, and your patent will be very valuable. If you don't, your patent could be worthless.

Since claims determine the scope of protection — what you can stop other people from doing — it's important that they find the right mix between being broad enough to cover design-arounds, yet narrow enough to be non-obvious and granted as a patent.

If I were writing a claim on an ebook reader it might look like this:

1. A method comprising:
loading at least one ebook into a memory of an ebook reader; and
displaying the at least one ebook via a display of the ebook reader.

Ignoring the novelty and obviousness issues, if this claim were granted in a utility patent, it would give the owner of that patent the right to exclude others from loading and displaying a book. That's very broad and would cover all ebook readers.

What if I wrote a claim on an ebook reader that instead looked like this:

1. A method comprising:
loading at least one ebook into a memory of an ebook reader; and
displaying the at least one ebook via a display of the ebook reader;
wherein the at least one ebook is displayed in Wingdings font.

Ignoring the novelty and obviousness issues, if this claim were granted in a utility patent, it would give the owner the right to exclude others from loading and displaying a book in Wingdings. This is very narrow and would cover almost no ebook readers.

The claims in a utility patent are like the roots of a tree. When people look at a tree, they see the branches and the leaves, but those can only exist with strong roots. If a tree has weak roots, it will topple.

Great patent attorneys consider ways that competitors can design around your invention to craft claims that preserve your rights. In many cases, an element of an invention that was thought to be rather unimportant later becomes a customers' favorite feature, and the thing that distinguishes them from their competitors.

Just because the cost of a feature is prohibitive today doesn't mean that an advance in technology, or a reduction in price, won't make that feature feasible in the future. If a competitor started making a competing device with those elements, would you want to compete with it?

Almost anyone can write a patent application that looks similar to a real patent application, but very few people can write claims that avoid pitfalls. Preparing an NPA without knowledge of what should be included, or excluded, from the claims is like planting a tree with shallow roots. It may look great at first glance, but it won't last, and it's not worth it.

*Strong claims*          *Weak claims*

Claims can be the difference between strong patent protection and a worthless stack of papers. A great patent attorney can help you craft a set of claims that fall into the former category.

### Business Card - Utility Patent
So let's go back to that business card. Is there something useful about the card? Does it have some function?

Yes. If you plant it in the dirt, it will grow a plant. Is that function novel and non-obvious?

No. Paper that has embedded seeds already exists. It's not novel. Business card shapes are widely known. Cutting this paper with embedded seeds into the shape of a business card is an obvious adjustment. It's not non-obvious. So, it wouldn't make sense for me to file a utility patent application on a business card constructed from paper with embedded seeds.

What if this business card had another feature? There is one very common complaint in the reviews of paper stock with embedded seeds.

"I planted the card, and nothing grew! What the heck?"

13

Let's say that I figured out a way to solve this problem. I *invented* a solution, which is to embed a particular fertilizer in the paper stock to provide nutrients for the seeds. This solution increases the grow rate of a planted card from a measly 35% to a whopping 88%!

Is this function novel and non-obvious? For this example, let's say it is. There are no paper stocks with embedded seeds that also contain fertilizers. It is novel. It would not have been obvious to one of ordinary skill in the art of paper with embedded seed manufacturing to use the particular fertilizer I created. It is non-obvious.

So, I can go ahead and protect my idea by filing a utility patent application with the goal of getting an issued utility patent.

### Other Examples of Utility Patents

Utility patents can include virtually anything useful: from mechanical inventions dreamed up in your garage to improvements on multi-million dollar equipment in a high-tech lab.

### Your Utility Patents

What are some inventions you have that are useful, novel, and non-obvious? These may include mechanical devices, software, improvements to existing inventions, etc. List them on the next page. If you're reading this on a borrowed copy or ebook, you can find a printable list at http://book.keytoip.com.

# Your
# Utility Patents

1. _____

_____

2. _____

_____

3. _____

_____

4. _____

_____

5. _____

_____

6. _____

_____

7. _____

_____

### Refining Questions

You may have a long list of potential utility patents. You may have a single great idea. So, how do you go about getting your utility patent(s)? There are a few options for going forward, and three questions can help you decide how to best proceed. First, is your invention complete or a work in progress? Second, do you want protection domestically or internationally? Third, do you want an issued patent fast or slow?

### Question One: Complete or Work in Progress?

This first question relates to where you are in the development of the invention. Why does this matter? Well, obtaining a utility patent takes a lot of time and money. You want to ensure that when you finally get a utility patent, it fully covers your invention. Remember that patents allow an inventor to exclude others. This is only useful if the utility patent covers something worth excluding.

#### Nonprovisional Patent Application (NPA)

Some people have a final version of their invention. There are no further improvements to make. I may have found the perfect mix of fertilizers to make my business (card) grow. My invention is complete. There is nothing more that I can improve upon.

If you are sure that you have a final version of your invention, then you should file a nonprovisional patent application. A nonprovisional patent application is examined by an Examiner at the USPTO and can issue as a utility patent if it's held to be novel and non-obvious.

#### Provisional Patent Application (PPA)

Other people may only have a prototype: a temporary solution. They could be actively working on developing new versions that are smaller, faster, cheaper, more efficient, etc. I may have created a prototype that grows the seeds when planted, but I think there is room for improvement.

Let's say that I've created a fertilizer that will grow the cards consistently, but I'm having trouble keeping it properly distributed. Some of my cards have a lot of fertilizer and grow lots of plants, while others have almost no fertilizer and produce nothing. This would be fine on a full letter-sized sheet of paper, but it gets exacerbated when on the much smaller surface area of a business card.

If you're still developing your invention, then you should file a provisional patent application. A provisional patent application is not examined or published. It gives you one year to develop your product or talk to investors. After a year, you have to file a nonprovisional patent application or let it go!

<u>Summary</u>

To summarize, if your invention is complete, file a nonprovisional patent application. If there's still work to be done on your invention, file a provisional patent application.

<u>Your List of Utility Patents</u>

Go to your list above and add a notation next to each potential utility patent. If it's complete write "(NPA)" for a nonprovisional patent application. If there is still work to be done, write "(PPA)" for a provisional patent application.

**Question Two: Domestic or International?**

The second question relates to where you want protection. The USPTO is only concerned with providing protection in the United States. A utility patent will only exclude others from making, using, selling, importing, or offering an invention for sale over a fixed period of time in the US. If I only want to protect my fertilizer seed card in the US, then I want a utility patent. But what if I want to protect my invention in Germany?

### Patent Cooperation Treaty (PCT)

Patent protection in other countries can be obtained through the filing a Patent Cooperation Treaty application, or PCT for short. A PCT application allows you to enter any of 151 contracting countries to obtain patent protection. It is examined, but it does not issue as a patent. Instead, you have to enter each desired member country individually, just as you would with the USPTO.

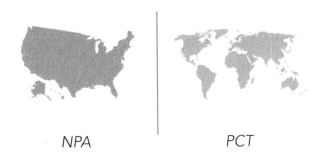

*NPA*                    *PCT*

A PCT doesn't mature into a patent but holds a spot in each country you want to file into. A PCT is like an RSVP for various countries that can be entered into to at a later time.

A PCT application offers an advantage over directly filing an initial application in each country as it lets you wait until thirty months, in most cases, after an initial filing before these individual countries filings must be completed.

An inventor can file a PCT application at any time within twelve months of an initial filing. So, if I file a nonprovisional patent application or a provisional patent application on my fertilizer seed invention on January 1, 2017, I have until January 1, 2018, to file a PCT application. I can use this time to gauge whether there is any international interest in this invention. Perhaps I find a sudden interest in fertilizer seed business cards in Italy. As long as it's been less than one year from any initial application filing, I can file a PCT application and seek protection in Italy, along with any of the other 150 countries that are part of the PCT.

Summary

To summarize, if you only want patent protection within the United States, then file a nonprovisional patent application or a provisional patent application. If you want patent protection in other countries, file a PCT application within a year of your initial nonprovisional patent application or a provisional patent application filing date.

Your List of Utility Patents

Go to your list above and add a second notation for international protection. If you want protection internationally, add "(PCT)" for the Patent Cooperation Treaty.

Remember that you have one year from a first filing in the US — either a provisional patent application or a nonprovisional patent application — to file a PCT application. You can use this time to seek funding and research the market before deciding whether international protection is worth the (big) cost.

**Question Three: Fast or Slow?**

This question may have been phrased as fast or regular speed. The truth is that the patent process is slow. The time from initial filing to when an Examiner at the USPTO looks at your application may be 2-4 years. For many people, this is not an issue. During the time that a patent application is pending, you can mark your products with the phrase "patent pending." While you can't enforce a patent application against infringers until it issues, it does put others on notice of your invention. Once your utility patent issues, any infringers will be liable for infringement during the time your application was pending.

Track One

There is also a faster way. If you need a patent quick because you have an active infringer, your investor wants it, you just don't want to wait, etc. then you can file what's known as a Track One application. For a hefty fee, the USPTO will allow you to skip the line with the goal of having a final resolution of your application within twelve months. This means that an Examiner at the USPTO may look at your application after only 2-4 months, rather than 2-4 years if filed regularly.

In addition to the hefty fee for filing quickly, there are additional costs to consider. If you file a Track One application, then you'll likely need the services of a patent attorney to respond to an Office action within 5-7 months after filing. If all goes well, you'll also have to pay the issue fees within twelve months. For many people, these short-term costs may be better utilized in growing other areas of the business.

Summary

To summarize, if you don't mind waiting, file a regular application and wait for your patent application to be examined. If you have an urgent need that justifies the extra cost, then go ahead and file a Track One application.

## Your List of Utility Patents

It's time to add a third notation to your list of potential utility patents. If you need a patent quickly, insert the notation "(TO)" for Track One.

You should now have a list of potential utility patents. For each item in this list you have an idea of whether you should start with a provisional or a nonprovisional patent application, seek protection in the United States or internationally, and file at the regular speed or with a Track One application. Treat this as an active list, and feel free to go back and add new items to it periodically. You may be surprised to find how many of your great ideas can be protected by utility patents.

# 3
# DESIGN PATENTS

## Overview

The second type of patent is a design patent. A design patent protects the aesthetic parts of an invention — what it looks like.

Design patents can be granted to anyone who invents a new, original, and ornamental design for an article of manufacture. If it's ornamental, it's a design patent.

To put it simply, design patents cannot have utility. Or, even more simply, design patents must literally be useless.

Just because a design patent must be useless, doesn't mean it lacks value. The look of a product can often be just as important as its use. A decorative vase, for example, may have a design that doesn't do anything — it's useless — but looks aesthetically pleasing and results in customers buying that vase.

**Filing Process**

Application > Examination > Issuance

Much like utility patents, there are limits on public disclosure, sale, and use before filing. Specifically, the design must not have been described in a publication, sold, offered for sale, or released more than one year before the date of the application.

An added benefit of design patents is that they tend to be simpler, less expensive, and faster to issue than utility patents. Design patents show a product in a series of drawings and have minimal accompanying text, which reduces the cost. A design patent may be issued within a year of filing as long as there aren't any issues with patentability.

Much like a utility patent, a design patent starts out as an application. A design patent application is filed, an Examiner at the USPTO determines if it is novel and non-obvious, and if it is, it issues as a design patent.

Novelty and Non-obviousness

As with utility patents, design patents must be both novel and non-obvious. This is applied in a slightly different way, but the concept remains. You cannot get a design patent on an object that is the same as an existing object, as this would not be novel.

You also cannot get a design patent on an object that is basically the same as an existing object combined with other existing objects. This would not be non-obvious.

**Design Patent Lifespan**

Unlike utility patents, which have a lifespan of twenty years from filing, design patents have a lifespan of fifteen years from issuance. As an added benefit, there are no maintenance fees for design patents.

## Design Patent Drawings

Remember that in a utility patent application, the claims are vital. In a design patent, the claim doesn't matter. It's a generic element. A design patent only has one claim, and that claim looks like this:

Claim: The ornamental design for a (whatever) as shown and described.

The claim essentially says: Look at the drawings. So, while claims are vital to a utility patent, drawings are paramount to a design patent.

In a design patent, drawings show each angle of a device. Broken lines can be used to indicate parts of the invention that are present, but not claimed.

Let's say that you got a patent on the device shown in Drawing A and your competitor creates the device shown in Drawing B. Does Drawing B infringe your Design Patent shown in Drawing A?

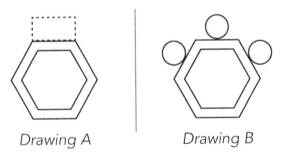

Drawing A          Drawing B

Yes, the device shown in Drawing B infringes your Design Patent. Every part of the device shown in solid

lines in Drawing A is present in Drawing B. The broken lines in Drawing A are not claimed, and so do not need to be present in infringing Drawing B.

### Business Card - Design Patent

Back to that plantable business card. Is there something useless about the card? What do you notice about its appearance?

It looks like an ordinary business card. If I were to file a design patent on this business card shape, it would be rejected as not novel.

What if I changed the shape of my business card to have a wavy shape along one side? As long as this shape is novel and non-obvious, I can get a design patent on the look of my business card. Then, I could exclude others from using that shape for fifteen years after that design patent issues.

### Other Examples of Design Patents

Design patents can cover uniquely shaped objects. They can also protect unique designs, patterns, or pictures applied to objects. Note that these designs, patterns, and pictures cannot be patented on their own, they need to be applied to an object to be covered by a design patent.

Design patents can also protect user interface layouts, icons, fonts, and animations used in electronics. Adobe, Apple, Facebook, Google, and others have all received design patents on user interfaces for their respective software products. Adobe has several design patents on font families. Apple has several design patents on their iOS keyboard, page turn, and swipe-to-unlock animations.

In addition to protecting unique products and unique objects applied to products, design patents can be used to protect a broad range of unique user interface elements.

### Your Design Patents

What are some of your products that have a unique design? List them on the next page.

# Your
# Design Patents

1. _____

_____

2. _____

_____

3. _____

_____

4. _____

_____

5. _____

_____

6. _____

_____

7. _____

_____

Many products can be protected by both utility patents and design patents. If an invention has both useful and ornamental features, then the useful features can be protected by a utility patent and the ornamental features can be protected by a design patent. How a phone works could be protected by utility patents while design patents could protect the phone's appearance.

Go back to your list of utility patents, and identify if any of them are products. For each product, think about whether they have a unique design or unique design elements. If they do, then add them to the above list.

# 4
# PLANT PATENTS

## Overview

I'm going to be honest. You probably don't need to learn about plant patents. Plant patents are only used in specific circumstances, and you will likely never need to protect a plant. The purpose of this book is to make you aware of all of the different types of intellectual property so that you can identify your intellectual property, protect it, and benefit from its value. That being said, if you had to skip one chapter, this would be the one to skip. See you at trademarks.

Are you still there? Good, then you're interested in learning more after we managed to *weed* out the people who didn't care. Did I write that first paragraph just so I could make a plant-based pun? Yes. I absolutely did. Now let's learn about plant patents.

Plant patents can be granted to anyone who invents or discovers and asexually reproduces any distinct and new variety of plant. This does not include edible tuber propagated plants, such as potatoes. A plant patent allows you to exclude others from asexually reproducing, selling, or using the protected plant.

If the plant was discovered, then the discovery must have been in a cultivated area. Asexual reproduction involves the propagation of a plant without the use of genetic seeds to create an exact genetic copy. Methods of asexual reproduction include rooting cuttings, grafting and budding, apomictic seeds, bulbs, division, slips, layering, rhizomes, runners, corms, tissue culture, and nucellar embryos.

### Filing Process

Much like utility patents and design patents, there are limits on public disclosure, sale, and use before filing. Specifically, the plant must not have been described in a publication, sold, offered for sale, or released more than one year before the date of the application.

An application for a plant patent is highly specific, and the use of an expert is encouraged. For example, the specification of a plant patent must include a detailed botanical description of the plant, which includes: genus and species; habit of growth; cultivar name; vigor; productivity; precocity, if applicable; botanical characteristics of plant structures such as buds, bark, foliage, flowers, and fruit; fertility; and any other characteristics which distinguish the plant such as resistance to disease, drought, cold, dampness, fragrance, coloration, regularity and time of bearing, quantity and quality of extracts, rooting ability, timing and duration of flowering season, etc.

An Examiner reviews the application for a plant patent at the USPTO. As with utility patents and design patents, the claimed plant must be both novel and non-obvious, though these are applied in a different way. If the Examiner does not object to the completeness of the botanical description and finds the plant both novel and non-obvious, then the application can issue as a plant patent.

### Plant Patent Lifespan

Much like utility patents, plant patents last for twenty years from the date of filing the application.

### Business Card - Plant Patent

This is where the plantable business card gets to shine. If the seeds in my plantable business card are for a plant protected by a plant patent, then my business card can grow a plant that is protected by a plant patent.

Note that most plantable paper contains seeds to grow wildflowers, which are not protected by plant patents.

### Your Plant Patents

List your invented or discovered, novel, non-obvious, and asexually reproduced plants on the next page.

In all likelihood, your list will be empty. That's perfectly reasonable. Now let's learn about Trademarks.

# Your
# Plant Patents

1. _____

   _____

2. _____

   _____

3. _____

   _____

4. _____

   _____

5. _____

   _____

6. _____

   _____

7. _____

   _____

# 5
# TRADEMARKS

**Overview**

You can think of trademarks as adjectives. Think of the space in front of a noun. How would you describe sneakers?

_____ *sneakers*

They could be *light* sneakers. They could be *colorful* sneakers. Or, they could be *Nike* sneakers. Nike is a trademark. It is used to distinguish the type of sneakers being sold. Just as you would use an adjective to describe a quality of an item, you can use a trademark to describe the source of that item.

A trademark gives you the right to keep others from using your adjective. Other companies can make light and colorful sneakers, but only Nike can make Nike sneakers.

This protection also applies to confusingly similar marks. So, not only does the Nike trademark keep others from making Nike sneakers, it keeps them from making Niike sneakers.

Specifically, a trademark is a word, name, symbol, or device that is used to indicate the source of goods or services and distinguish them from the goods or services of others.

### Trademark v Servicemark v Mark

Technically, trademarks are for goods, while servicemarks are for services. However, the term trademark is often used to refer to both trademarks and servicemarks. The term mark is short for both.

### Word mark v Design mark

Trademarks can be either word marks or stylized marks. Word marks are merely text with no claim to any particular font style, size, or color. Stylized marks may include some decoration, design elements, color, or even include the font used with text.

*Word mark*            *Stylized mark*

For many companies, it may make sense to trademark both a name, as a word mark and a logo of that name, as a stylized mark.

**Filing Process**
Common law v Federal registration
Trademarks are created automatically based on use in commerce. If you use a trademark in commerce, e.g., to sell goods or services, but have not filed for trademark protection with the USPTO, then you may have common law rights. Common law rights offer you some protection on the use of your trademark within the particular geographic area its being used.

So, if Kenny opened Kenny's Fried Chicken in Des Moines, IA and only sold his chicken in Iowa, then Kenny would have common law rights to "Kenny's Fried Chicken" in the geographic location of Iowa. But if he wants to open up a second branch in Anchorage, AK, he would have no rights his common law trademark in Alaska. If another Kenny, let's say Kenny G. (no relation), already opened a "Kenny's Fried Chicken" in Alaska, then Kenny from Iowa won't be able to expand his business to the land of Seward's Folly unless he chooses a new name.

Federal registration of your trademark, via the USPTO,

has numerous benefits over common law trademark rights. A registered trademark includes:

- A legal presumption of your ownership of your trademark and your exclusive rights to use your trademark nationwide.
- The public is put on notice of your claim to own your trademark.
- Your trademark is listed and searchable on the USPTO website.
- You can record your registration with Customs to prevent the importation of infringing foreign goods.
- You can use the symbol ®.
- You can sue someone in federal court for infringing your trademark.
- You can use your registration as a basis to obtain trademark protection in foreign countries.

None of these are possible with a common law trademark.

Obtaining a federal trademark registration is often a much quicker process than getting a utility patent. Once the application is filed, it will be assigned to a trademark Examiner. The Examiner will review your application to determine whether it is allowable. If the Examiner finds any problems, he or she will issue an Office action with a deadline of six months to respond. One of the most common reasons for an Office action is to amend the description of goods and services.

Once the Examiner finds no further issues, the trademark will be published. This starts a thirty-day window from publication for anyone else to oppose the registration. Think of it as the cliché moment in a movie where the officiator at a wedding says "speak now or forever hold your peace." If there are no objections, the trademark will receive a notice of allowance. Upon submitting an accepted statement of use in commerce, the trademark will be federally registered, and you can enjoy all of the benefits listed above.

Trademark Symbols (TM, SM, and ® )

You can, and should, use the appropriate symbol with your trademarks to put others on notice that you are claiming rights to your trademark. The symbol TM goes with an unregistered trademark for goods. The symbol SM works with an unregistered servicemark for services. The symbol ® goes with a trademark registered with the USPTO. The symbol ® is usually placed in superscript in the upper right-hand corner of your trademark, but this exact location is not required.

Use-in-commerce v intent-to-use

If you are already using a trademark and have common law rights, you can file for a registered trademark as a 'use-in-commerce' application. What if you haven't started using your trademark in commerce and you have no common law rights?

If you have a bona fide intent to use a trademark, i.e., you have a good faith intent to use a trademark and are not merely blocking a competitor from using it, then you can file an 'intent-to-use' application. This type of application can be useful to secure your trademark rights before launching a product or service with your trademark while you develop your business. Once your 'intent-to-use' application receives a notice of allowance, you have up to three years to file proof showing a use of your mark in commerce.

**Trademark Lifespan**

Declarations

Unlike patents, trademarks can last forever as long as

they continue to be used in commerce and you file the appropriate declarations. Declarations to allege continued use must be filed five years after the trademark is registered, and then every ten years after that.

### Business Card – Trademark
What are the trademarks on my business card?

The front of my business card has a logo. This logo has the words Key to IP integrated with a lightbulb and a key. It is being used for goods, such as this book, and so it is a trademark. If it were instead being used for legal services, then it would be a servicemark. I could use the symbol ™ to put others on notice that I claim to own this trademark. If I get this trademark registered, then I could add the symbol ® next to my trademark.

Because this logo uses a specific fonts and has several design elements it is a stylized mark instead of a word mark.

### Other Examples of Trademarks
Trademarks can include product or business names, but they can also include slogans. Look at some of your favorite products or services, and you'll likely see

trademark symbols next to their product name as well next to slogans.

**Your Trademarks**

What are some trademarks you have? Be sure to include any current business names, slogans, product names, or services. You can also list any business names, slogans, product names, or services that you intend to use in the future. List them on the next page.

# Your
# Trademarks

1. _____

   _____

2. _____

   _____

3. _____

   _____

4. _____

   _____

5. _____

   _____

6. _____

   _____

7. _____

   _____

## Trademark Categories

Once you have your list of trademarks, you'll want to determine the strength of each of them. Trademarks fall into one of five categories sorted by strength. The first two categories, generic and descriptive, are not able to be registered as trademarks. The latter three categories, suggestive, arbitrary, and fanciful, are inherently distinctive, and can be registered as trademarks. Let's go through each category, and you can identify which of the trademarks on your list above fall into which category.

### Generic

A trademark can not protect names that fall into the generic category. You can't trademark Soda brand soda because soda is a generic name used by everyone to refer to that category.

This is also the category where formerly strong trademarks go to die. If a company doesn't properly label and enforce their trademark, a court can rule that it has become generic.

Aspirin used to be a trademark held by Bayer that has since become generic in the United States. Bayer did not stop others from using the name aspirin to refer to acetylsalicylic acid (ASA), and so aspirin became the generic name. Other former trademarks that have become genericized include: cellophane, dry ice, escalator, heroin, kerosene, laundromat, linoleum, thermos, trampoline, and videotape.

You may have seen a news article where a company aggressively sends out cease-and-desist letters for improper use of their trademark. While such stories often portray the company as being too harsh, the reality is that these actions are necessary to prevent their trademark from becoming generic. A company has to enforce their trademark rights against others, or their trademark will eventually become generic.

For example, Google likely does not want people to refer to searching as "google it" (lowercase g) because it could lead to Google being seen as a generic trademark for any searching. Instead, Google likely wants people to use the Google (uppercase G) search engine.

A company may get excited about the idea of the media using their trademark as a go-to description of a field. However, that company needs to balance the advantage of the positive publicity with the risk that their trademark could be diluted and eventually become generic.

If a trademark is generic, it no longer indicates the source of goods. It indicates the category of goods.

Go through your list above and identify any of your trademarks that fit into this generic category. Then, cross out the names that fall into this category. A trademark cannot protect them.

### Descriptive

Names that fall into the descriptive category usually cannot be protected by a trademark. Descriptive trademarks describe an ingredient, quality, characteristic, function, feature, purpose, or use of the specified goods.

While Soda brand soda is a generic trademark, Energy brand soda is a descriptive trademark, because "energy" is a feature of the ingredients in soda.

Now I said that descriptive trademarks generally cannot be protected by a trademark because there is one exception. A descriptive trademark can acquire a secondary meaning when it comes to identify not only the goods but also the source of those goods.

How does a trademark acquire a secondary meaning? By showing that the primary significance of the trademark in the minds of the consuming public is the source of the goods, and not the goods themselves.

For example, International Business Machines is a company that provides international business machine hosting and consulting services. However, we as the public know them as IBM. When someone says IBM we think primarily of the company IBM rather than international business machines in general.

It is not recommended to pursue a descriptive trademark because you will likely not be able to register these names as trademarks. Go to your list of trademarks above and cross out any names that fall into the descriptive category.

Suggestive
There is a big gap between descriptive trademarks and suggestive trademarks.

*Generic*
*Descriptive*

*Suggestive*
*Arbitrary*
*Fanciful*

Descriptive trademarks immediately tell a consumer something about the goods. Suggestive trademarks require a little more imagination. Specifically, suggestive trademarks require imagination, thought, or perception to ascertain the nature of the goods covered by the trademark.

If Soda brand soda is generic and Energy brand soda is descriptive, then Hummingbird brand soda is suggestive as hummingbirds are associated with having high energy.

Suggestive trademarks, like arbitrary and fanciful trademarks, are considered inherently distinctive and do not require evidence of acquired distinctiveness.

Go to your list of trademarks and note any suggestive trademarks with an "(S)". Suggestive trademarks can be especially useful to a new or small business because they have some relation to the products or services being sold. Just make sure that they require enough imagination to keep from being confused for descriptive trademarks.

Arbitrary

Arbitrary trademarks include common words in a surprising context. It's words you wouldn't traditionally associate with certain products or services. An arbitrary trademark does not suggest or describe a significant ingredient, quality, or characteristic of the goods.

As a Hummingbird brand soda is a suggestive trademark, a Moon brand soda is an arbitrary trademark. Moon is a common word used in the surprising context of soda.

A trademark is tied to goods and services, so while arbitrary trademarks can be generic for one type of good or service, they can be arbitrary for another. For example, Apple is used as a trademark for computers and a record label. Apple, the fruit, does not suggest or describe a significant ingredient, quality, or characteristic of computers or a record label. Therefore, Apple is an arbitrary, and inherently distinctive, trademark.

What about if someone wanted to make Apple brand apples? Apple brand apples would be a generic trademark because they describe the type of goods. Generic trademarks are not given trademark protection.

Go to your list and note any arbitrary trademarks with an "(A)." If you had accidentally crossed out any arbitrary trademarks as generic trademarks, now is the time to correct this.

### Fanciful

Fanciful trademarks are words invented for the sole purpose of identifying the source of goods. It's an entirely new made up word.

For example, Kodak is a fanciful trademark. George Eastman, the founder of Kodak, said that a brand name should be short, easy to pronounce and not resemble any other name. That last quality is what makes a trademark a fanciful trademark.

While a Hummingbird brand soda is a suggestive mark, a Ddsdfdesdfsf brand soda is a fanciful mark. Although, like the Welsh town of Llanfairpwllgwyngyllgogerychwyrn-drobwllllantysiliogogogoch, it is neither short nor easy pronounce.

Go to your list of trademarks and identify any fanciful trademarks with an "(F)." Fanciful marks have the advantage of being new and avoiding confusion with existing marks. The disadvantage of using a fanciful mark is that — in the beginning — it doesn't have any relation to your product. When starting a new business, it may take a lot more marketing to establish a fanciful mark than a suggestive mark that has some relation to your goods or services.

If any trademarks are remaining, ones that don't have notations or aren't already crossed out, then try and sort those into one of the five trademark categories. You may find that some trademarks are 'on the fence' between descriptive and suggestive. Make sure that any suggestive trademarks truly require imagination so that you don't end up pursuing a descriptive trademark that is unlikely to be registered.

### Trademark Search

Once you find your ideal trademark, you need to make sure no one else is already using it. This helps avoid a "likelihood of confusion" with other trademarks.

A trademark search can be used to prevent a likelihood of confusion with other trademarks. How do you determine a likelihood of confusion? You look for similar trademarks with related goods and services. So, two identical, or similar trademarks can co-exist as long as the goods and services are not related, such as Apple music company and Apple computers.

Here are several sources to start on a preliminary search for your trademark:

- Trademark Electronic Search System (TESS) at http://tess.uspto.gov
- General Internet Search at http://www.google.com
- Domain Name Search at http://www.instantdomainsearch.com
- Yelp Business Listings at http://www.yelp.com
- Yellow Pages Business Listings at http://yellowpages.superpages.com
- Facebook Search at http://www.facebook.com
- Historical Website Search at http://www.archive.org
- Amazon Product Search at http://www.amazon.com
- eBay Product Search at http://www.ebay.com

As you go through your search, you may find other product names, business names, or slogans that look similar to your proposed trademark. One consideration should be how similar these are to your proposed trademark. If there are any similar trademarks, you should check to make sure that the goods and services of this similar trademark do not overlap with your proposed trademark.

If there are identical trademarks with similar goods and services, consider crossing these trademarks off of your list. If there are similar trademarks with similar goods and services, add a "(?)" to your trademark on your list and know to proceed with caution.

Another practical consideration should be who owns those similar trademarks. If a Fortune 500 company holds a similar trademark, there is a much higher likelihood that this company may oppose your trademark, even if the goods and services are wildly different. You may decide that your resources are better spent growing your business than fighting a battle with a company that has deep pockets.

If a large company owns a similar trademark add a "(*)" to your trademark on your list and know to proceed with caution.

# 6
# COPYRIGHTS

**Overview**

A copyright protects a work of authorship fixed in a tangible medium of expression. Copyrights do not protect ideas, but they can protect how those ideas are expressed.

Copyrights can include a multitude of forms including literary, dramatic, musical, and artistic works, such as poetry, novels, movies, songs, computer software, and architecture. A single word or sentence is not significant enough to be a work of authorship. Something like a company name, title, short phrase, or slogan is better protected with a trademark.

A work that literally copies the fixed work of authorship is infringing. However, a work that is not literally identical, but uses significant portions can also be infringing.

The general rule is that the person who creates a work is the owner of that work. An exception to this general rule is works made for hire. A work made for hire is a piece of work prepared by an employee within the scope of his or her employment or work specially ordered or commissioned. The owner of a work made for hire is the employer or commissioning party.

So, if you write a book on your own, then you are the owner of your book. If you write a book as part of your job writing books at We Write Books, Inc., then We Write Books, Inc. is the owner. If you write a book about Chris Weiss, which is commissioned by Chris Weiss and includes a provision that the book is a work made for hire, then Chris Weiss is the owner. For the book you are reading, Key to IP, I have written this book on my own, and thus I am the owner.

Copyright Notice

You can mark each copyrighted item with a copyright notice. A copyright notice is not required, because copyright is automatic once a work is fixed in a tangible medium. However, a copyright notice informs the public that a work is protected, identifies the owner, and shows the year of first publication.

So what does a copyright notice look like? There are three elements. First, the symbol © (a letter c in a circle), the word "Copyright" or the abbreviation "Copr." Second, the year of first publication. Third, the name of the copyright owner. The owner can be a person or company name. In an audio recording, this notice may be spoken.

Fair Use

One issue that comes up a lot in copyright cases is fair use. In some circumstances, a copyright may be used for purposes such as criticism, comment, news reporting, teaching, scholarship, or research, and such uses are not an infringement of copyright. Fair use is always decided on a case-by-case basis, which means that there are no formulas you can use to determine with certainty whether something is fair use or not. Instead, four factors are considered.

The first factor is the purpose and character of the use, including whether such use is of a commercial nature or is for nonprofit educational purposes. The second factor is the nature of the copyrighted work. The third factor is the amount and substantiality of the portion used in relation to the copyrighted work as a whole. The fourth factor is the effect of the use upon the potential market for or value of the copyrighted work.

Since the use of a copyrighted work can only be deemed as fair use by a court, it is best to avoid or limit using copyrighted works owned by large or litigious companies. If you still want to proceed, it is best to talk to an intellectual property attorney who can give you advice that matches your particular circumstances.

### Filing Process

Copyrights are unique as compared to patents and trademarks because you don't need to register a copyright to have it exist. Copyright is created on its own. In fact, a copyright exists from the moment the work is fixed in a tangible form that it is perceptible. Works floating in your mind do not qualify for copyright protection.

Copyrights don't need to be registered. However, copyrights can be registered, and registration offers advantages. A registered copyright puts others on notice of your rights to a work of authorship. Additionally, your copyright needs to be registered before you can bring a lawsuit for infringement of your copyright.

Filing for a registered copyright is a relatively simple process as compared to patents and trademarks. You only need a completed copyright application, the work to be registered, and a filing fee. The processing time for an electronically filed copyright is about 6-10 months. So long as there aren't any issues, you will receive a registration certificate and registration number for your copyright.

You may have heard some people refer to a "poor man's copyright." This usually involves someone mailing themselves a copy of their work. The idea is that the mailing date stamped on the sealed envelope can be used to prove that the work sealed inside was created on a certain date. This is a myth, and there is no legal protection for such an act. Registering a copyright can cost as low as $35, which means there is no excuse for not doing it the right, and legally valid, way.

### Copyright Lifespan

Copyright lasts a long time. For new works, copyright

protection lasts for the life of the author plus an additional 70 years.

So, if a man publishes a book called "How to Live Forever" in 2017 and ends up dying in one hundred years at the rather disappointing age of 117, then the copyright on "How to live Forever" will remain in effect until 2187. Although, to be honest, what's the point?

If the copyright is a work made for hire, then copyright protection lasts for 95 years from the year of its first publication or 120 years from the year of its creation, whichever expires first.

If that same man wrote his book "How to Live Forever" as a work made for hire, and it was first published in 2017, then the copyright on "How to Live Forever" would remain in effect until a much-more-reasonable 2112. If, however, this book was completed in 2017 but not published until 2136, copyright protection would only last until 2137.

If the above math has you a bit confused, I can summarize copyright lifespan with this: copyright lasts a very, very, very long time.

### Business Card – Copyright
Let's revisit that business card. We've already discussed how utility patents, design patents, plant patents, and trademarks could protect this deceivingly simple object. Could this business card also be protected by copyright?

Remember that names, titles, short phrases, and slogans are not copyrightable. Trademarks can be used to protect these elements. Let's turn that business card around.

How to make your card grow:
*1 - Place this card in firm, but not packed, soil*
*2 - Place an 1/8" layer of soil over this card*
*3 - Water this card whenever the soil feels dry*
*4 - Enjoy your flowers*

**KEY**

How to make your business grow:
*1 - Learn about Intellectual Property at keytoip.com*

On the back of this business card are instructions for how to plant this business card and make plants grow from the seeds within. Planting instructions are nothing new. However, copyright doesn't have to cover new material. It just has to present this material in a new way. Copyrights do not protect ideas, but they can protect how those ideas are expressed.

Let's say that my planting instructions are well-known, but the way that I've written out these instructions is brand new. As these instructions have been 'published' in a tangible medium, they are subject to copyright. Copyright is automatic.

What if I wanted to register my copyright on these planting instructions? If I were worried about rival plantable business card companies stealing my instructions verbatim, I could file for a registered copyright. However, all that would be needed to avoid this copyright would be to reword my directions in a new way.

**Other Examples of Copyrights**

You may have some copyrights related to your product, company, and even fundraising efforts. Let's identify a few of these.

If your product includes software that accomplishes several tasks, it has an underlying source code. Copyright protects this source code itself.

You may have a product manual that lets your customers know how to set up your product, answers some common questions, and provides contact information for follow-ups. Copyright protects this product manual.

If you decide to raise money for your business you may meet with some investors and show them a presentation that breaks down your product, the market for your product, and your business plans moving forward. This presentation, along with any audio, video, or other components contained in the presentation, is protected by copyright.

The number of materials subject to copyright will invariably increase as time goes on. If you conduct market research, create a product website, create an advertisement to sell your product, or create a database of customer information, then these new works will also be protected by copyright.

### Your Copyrights

What are some copyrights you have? Be sure to include any copyrights that you intend to create in the future. List them on the next page.

# Your Copyrights

1. _____

   _____

2. _____

   _____

3. _____

   _____

4. _____

   _____

5. _____

   _____

6. _____

   _____

7. _____

   _____

Go to your list of copyrights and identify any copyrights that are, or will be, a work-for-hire. Identify these copyrights by adding "(WFH)."

Go back to your list of copyrights and identify any works that you want to register with the copyright office. This should include any works that are at an elevated risk for being copied. For example, a product manual for a device that has a large number of copycats. Identify these copyrights by adding "(R)."

Since copyright is created automatically, it is important to go back to this list frequently and ensure that your copyrights are being properly identified and protected.

# 7
# TRADE SECRETS

## Overview

A trade secret is made up of secret, valuable, and protected information. Unlike other forms of intellectual property, trade secrets are not registered. Instead of being published, trade secrets are simply kept secret. Trade secrets are like the official form of the secret family cookie recipe passed down through generations.

Some examples of well-known trade secrets include Google's search algorithm, the ingredients in WD-40, the eleven herbs and spices used by Colonel Sanders in KFC, and the formula for Coca-Cola. Each of these well-known trade secrets is made up of secret, valuable, and protected information.

### Secret

Let's look at the first element: secret. Secret just means that the information is not known to the public. If information has already been widely disclosed, then it can't be a trade secret. It's literally the second word.

### Valuable

The second aspect, valuable, is a little more nuanced. The information itself must derive its value from not being publicly known.

If someone steals the Mona Lisa, then that is theft, but it is not theft of a trade secret. The Mona Lisa does not derive economic value from being secret to the public, but from being the Mona Lisa. However, if that Mona Lisa had the formula for Coca-Cola written on the back of it in permanent marker, then that would also be theft of a trade secret. If the information would lose its value upon being revealed, then it is considered valuable as a trade secret.

Coca-Cola is worth more than store-brand cola, *because* of its unique flavor. Remember that Coca-Cola doesn't have a utility patent on its secret formula. If that formula were revealed, then anyone could make Coca-Cola, including generic cola. At that point, the flavor of both colas would be identical, and people might choose generic cola over Coca-Cola.

### Protected

Which brings us to the last aspect of a trade secret: protected. Specifically, a trade secret must have reasonable measures taken to protect the secret and valuable information. Reasonable measures mean taking enough steps to prevent revealing the secret and valuable information.

For KFC, reasonable measures meant storing the Colonel's recipe on a piece of paper locked in a 770 pound high-tech safe, encased in two feet of concrete, and surrounded by 24-hour video and motion detection surveillance. For other companies, reasonable measures are a little more *reasonable*.

You can think of trade secrets like a fenced off area. The protection is the fence itself. The secret and valuable information is what is stored behind the fence. Now, not all fences are the same. Some have gaps, which can reveal what's behind them. Others fences are sturdier, and do a better job of keeping people from looking in.

As a business grows, the amount of information that could qualify as a trade secret also grows. It is important to establish policies that adapt and grow with this information.

### Filing Process

There is no filing process for trade secrets. Trade secrets are created by taking reasonable measures to protect secret and valuable information.

Even though there is no official filing process, if a competitor divulges your trade secrets through illegal means, such as theft or social engineering, they can be punished in a court of law.

### Trade Secret Lifespan

As long as the valuable information is kept secret, it can remain a trade secret. This means that trade secrets can last forever.

### Business Card - Trade Secret

My business card encompasses utility patents, design patents, plant patents, trademarks, and copyrights, but does it also include any trade secrets? How would you even know?

Let's say that I found a manufacturer to print my business cards with a particular fertilizer embedded into the card. There are hundreds, if not thousands, of companies that could print these cards, but the one I found has the best mix of cost and quality. Is the identity of this manufacturer a trade secret? To be so, it has to be secret, valuable, and protected.

First, is it a secret? Let's say that I haven't told anyone about the manufacturer I am using. It isn't known, so it's a secret. Second, is it valuable? If someone else wanted to make a competing plantable business card, then knowing the identity of this manufacturer would allow them to source cards at a competitive price and quality level. Therefore, the identity of the manufacturer is valuable, because it is a secret. Third, is it protected? Let's say I keep the identity of the manufacturer in a password protected folder on a password protected computer. These are reasonable measures, so it is protected.

Therefore, the identity of my plantable business card manufacturer is a trade secret and will remain a trade secret until one of the elements is no longer met.

### Other Examples of Trade Secrets

I used several examples of large enterprises having high-profile trade secrets. However, the reality is that most trade secrets are a little more mundane.

Trade secrets can include any information that is secret and valuable. For a business this can include:
- Customer data
- Computer programs
- Financial records
- Future products or services
- Marketing plans
- Raw data
- Schematics
- Source code

- Supplier identities
- Research & development plans

If a competitor obtained this information, they could use it to poach customers, change their strategy, and get necessary components to build copycat products or services.

**Your Trade Secrets**

What is some secret, valuable, and protected information that you have? List your trade secrets on the next page. Then, tear it out and store it in a safe place.

# Your
# Trade Secrets

1. _____
   _____

2. _____
   _____

3. _____
   _____

4. _____
   _____

5. _____
   _____

6. _____
   _____

7. _____
   _____

### Reviewing your Patents, Trademarks, and Copyrights

Trade secrets can also include any unfiled or unpublished items on the lists you created for utility patents, design patents, plant patents, trademarks, and copyrights.

For example, until you file a utility patent application on your invention, that invention is a trade secret, i.e., it contains secret, valuable, and protected information. The same goes for trademarks you are planning to use and copyrights before they are published. If a competitor found out about your plans to file patent applications, use trademarks, or publish copyrighted material, then they could take actions to weaken your business.

Go back through your lists for utility patents, design patents, plant patents, trademarks, and copyrights and add any secret and unpublished items to your list of trade secrets. Treating these things as trade secrets, and using reasonable measures to protect against their discovery, is a good habit for any inventor or business.

### Reasonable Measures

You must take reasonable measures to protect your secret and valuable information if you want to turn it into trade secrets. So what is a reasonable measure?

For KFC, it was building a high-tech safe. For you, it can be as simple as a password. Starting out, you can encrypt your files so that someone else, legally or not, cannot access them.

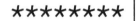

*Password must be at least eight characters, include a number,
an uppercase letter, a non-standard character, and a haiku.*

As your business grows, you can add additional measures to secure your secret and valuable information. For example, when you present this information to a supplier, you can have them sign a non-disclosure agreement (NDA), when you hire an employee you can have the employment agreement specify what information is a trade secret and what steps the employee has to take to safeguard this information, and-if it comes to it-you can even put a safe with 24/7 surveillance in your corporate headquarters for any especially vital information.

There is no one-size-fits-all approach to trade secrets, but being proactive about protection can ensure that any secret and valuable information stays that way.

### Reverse Engineering

Reverse engineering is the process of disassembling something to learn how it works. The component suppliers for a computer could be held as a trade secret but would be discovered as soon as someone takes the computer apart to find its parts.

The possibility of reverse engineering is an important consideration in choosing between a trade secret and a utility patent. A utility patent has a limited lifetime as compared to the potentially infinite lifetime of a trade secret. However, a trade secret loses its protection once it is no longer a secret. If a product can be reverse engineered, then it may make more sense to protect the product with a utility patent.

In practice, the distinction between utility patents and trade secrets is not as black and white. There are often some components of an invention that can be easily reverse engineered and would be better protected by a utility patent. There may be other elements of the invention which cannot be or are not easily, reverse engineered. The easily reverse engineered elements can be protected with a utility patent, while the hideable elements can be protected as a trade secret.

Go to your list of trade secrets above and note whether any of them could be easily reverse engineered. If they can be reverse engineered, then consider moving them to your list for Utility Patents.

# 8
# CONCLUSION

"So that's it," I say. "You now have a list of your potential utility patents, design patents, plant patents, trademarks, copyrights, and trade secrets."

"Thanks," you respond. "That was very useful."

"I'm glad I could –"

"Except for that part about plant patents," you interject. "I found that to be boring and unnecessary."

"Most people don't use them, but I wanted to be complete," I say.

You look down and notice that your plate of glazed chicken skewers has gone cold. "So if I have an idea for a plate that keeps your food warm –"

"While you end up in a long conversation with someone about intellectual property," I say.

"Exactly. Then, I can protect the useful elements with a utility patent and the overall look with a design patent."

"That's correct," I say.

"The product name and slogans can be protected by trademarks. Oh, and any marketing copy I create for the Plateizator 1000 can be protected by copyright."

"Plateizator 1000?"

"It's a working title," you say. "A rough draft. My overall marketing plan for the Plateizator 1000 including supplier and market research on my customers can be covered by trade secrets. So that uses everything. Except plant patents. Which seem useless."

"They're not for everyone," I say. "Intellectual property is like a set of tools, and this conversation lets you know which ones to select. A utility patent is like a hammer, a design patent is like a wrench, and a plant patent —"

"Is like a Halligan Bar," you suggest.

"Sure," I say, making a mental note to look that up in the Google search engine later.

"It's hard to know where to start," you admit. "Not knowing whether I need a patent or a copyright is like buying a book on advanced hammer techniques and spending twelve hours reading it only to find out that I should have purchased a book on introductory lathing."

"That's a good analogy," I say. "You now have the tools for protecting your great ideas. What you build with those tools is up to you."

"Thanks again."

"Glad to help." I begin to walk away.

"One last thing," you request. "Got any tips for networking?"

"Not a one," I respond with a smile. "Good luck."

You look over the lists you've created. You now have an understanding of the different types of intellectual property and are better prepared to identify new areas of protection. If you need to do more research, you now know what you're looking for. You have the tools. And that's when you have a great idea.

# RESOURCES

Congratulations! You've finished this book. Whether you're a CEO or a secretary, work at a Fortune 500 company or work at a start-up, reading this book has prepared you to identify patents, trademarks, copyrights, and trade secrets.

Now what? The lessons you've absorbed in these pages mean that you now know 90% more than the general public. You could use this information to stop others from copying an exciting new product line (utility patent), create a strong name for your business (trademark), and ensure that customer information stays safe (trade secret). What you do with your new skills depends on your needs.

Below is a list of resources that can help you increase the solid base of information you've already built. You can use these resources to help hire the right attorney for your needs, learn the step-by-step of how to file certain types of intellectual property, and further your knowledge.

## USPTO: Manual of Patent Examining Procedure (MPEP)

The MPEP contains all of the laws and regulations that must be followed during the patent process. This document is very technical and does not make for fun reading. However, the information contained inside can be very useful if you know where to look. If you printed out a full version of the MPEP, it would use up 4,106 pages. I'd recommend sticking to the online version.

https://www.uspto.gov/web/offices/pac/mpep/

## USPTO: Inventors Assistance Center (IAC)

The Inventors Assistance Center (IAC) is a toll-free phone line you can call for answers to your patent questions. They can answer general questions, assist you with forms, and direct you to additional information. They cannot provide legal advice or tell you whether an invention is patentable. The IAC a great place to start if you have a question, but aren't sure about the next step.

Toll-Free: 1-800-786-9199

https://www.uspto.gov/learning-and-resources/support-centers/inventors-assistance-center-iac

## USPTO: Nonprovisional (Utility) Patent Application Filing Guide

The USPTO provides a short guide on how to file a Utility Patent application.

https://www.uspto.gov/patents-getting-started/patent-basics/types-patent-applications/nonprovisional-utility-patent

## USPTO: A Guide to Filing A Design Patent Application

The USPTO provides a short guide on how to file a Design Patent application.

https://www.uspto.gov/web/offices/com/iip/pdf/brochure_05.pdf

## USPTO Public Patent Application Information Retrieval (PAIR)

Public PAIR provides the status and underlying documents for publicly available patents and applications. Reviewing these documents can be especially useful if you want to see why an application was allowed or abandoned. Once you select an application, you can click on the "Image File Wrapper" tab, which will let you see any Office actions, arguments used in Office action responses, claim amendments, and reasons for Notices of Allowance. Reading through these documents can familiarize you with the patent process.

http://portal.uspto.gov/pair/PublicPair

## Patent Search

The USPTO provides a way to search published patent applications and issued patents, but the user interface leaves much to be desired. Services such as Free Patents Online allow you to search by patent number as well as keywords, assignee, inventors, etc. For example, to find patents owned by Google you could search "AN/Google." Reading through these issued patents can help you to familiarize yourself with the format used in patent applications.

http://www.freepatentsonline.com

## WIPO Patentscope

This website allows you to search Patent Cooperation Treaty (PCT) applications. Once you select a PCT application, the "Documents" tab can be used to view the International Search Report (ISR), which is similar to an Office action in the United States.

https://patentscope.wipo.int/search/en/search.jsf

## USPTO: Trademark Manual of Examining Procedure (TMEP)

The TMEP contains all of the laws and regulations that must be followed during filing and maintaining a trademark. As with the MPEP, this document is very technical. If you printed out a full version of the TMEP, it would use a much more reasonable 1,422 pages.

https://tmep.uspto.gov/RDMS/TMEP/current

## USPTO Trademark ID Manual

This website can be used to search USPTO's ID Manual for acceptable identifications of goods and services. Type in a term to describe your goods and services, and it will provide a list of identifications along with their class, status, type, and any notes. Statuses of A, M, or X are usually acceptable, while a status of D is generally not acceptable.

https://tmidm.uspto.gov/id-master-list-public.html

## USPTO Trademark Status & Document Retrieval (TSDR)

This website is the equivalent of Public PAIR for Trademarks. You can view the status, goods and services, owner information, etc. of pending or registered trademarks. Under the 'Documents' tab, you can see any Office actions, arguments in Office actions responses, Examiner amendments, etc.

https://tsdr.uspto.gov

## USPTO Fee Schedule

This page lists the latest government fees for patents and trademarks. Please note that the cost for filing a patent includes the basic filing fee, search fee, and examination fee.

https://www.uspto.gov/learning-and-resources/fees-and-payment/uspto-fee-schedule

## USPTO Patent Forms

This webpage provides links to all of the forms used in filing a patent application.

https://www.uspto.gov/patent/forms/forms-patent-applications-filed-or-after-september-16-2012

## USPTO Newsletter

The USPTO provides an irregularly published newsletter called Inventors Eye. It contains stories, advice, and tips for independent inventors.

https://www.uspto.gov/learning-and-resources/newsletter-archives-old

## The United States Copyright Office: A Guide to Filing an Electronic Copyright Registration

This step-by-step guide shows you have to file an

electronic copyright registration. Screenshots and annotations of each step make the copyright filing process easy to follow.

https://www.copyright.gov/eco/eco-tutorial-standard.pdf

### Intellectual Property History

This page provides information on famous patents, trademarks, and copyrights for each day of the year. While this won't help you to file your applications, it can provide some inspiration or a good trivia fact.

http://inventors.about.com/od/todayinhistory/qt/day_in_history.htm

### Nolo Do-It-Yourself Books

Nolo provides a series of step-by-step books for filing patents, trademarks, and copyrights. These can be very helpful for people who can't afford a lawyer or just want to learn more about the filing process itself. Be warned that special considerations unique to your great idea or business cannot be uniformly addressed in any book. While many people have saved money by going the DIY route, others have lost valuable intellectual property or opened themselves up to needless litigation. Be sure to check your local library to see if they have access to the book you are interested in reading. For example, library patrons in Los Angeles County can get free electronic access to many Nolo books on intellectual property.

http://store.nolo.com/products/intellectual-property
http://search.ebscohost.com/login.aspx?authtype=custuid&custid=ns129672

### Frequently Asked Questions (FAQs)

If you have an intellectual property question, chances are you're not the first. These FAQs may provide you with an answer to your question. I'd recommend searching for certain keywords rather than reading these through in a linear order.

https://www.uspto.gov/learning-and-resources/general-faqs

https://www.uspto.gov/help/patent-help

http://www.wipo.int/patents/en/faq_patents.html

https://www.uspto.gov/learning-and-resources/trademark-faqs

http://www.wipo.int/trademarks/en/

https://www.copyright.gov/help/faq/

http://www.wipo.int/copyright/en/faq_copyright.html

# ABOUT THE AUTHOR

Chris Weiss is an intellectual property attorney admitted to practice before the United States Patent and Trademark Office and all courts of the State of California. His background allows him to create the strongest possible patent by approaching details beyond a traditional engineering lens. Chris has degrees in business, psychology, and law, which offers him a comprehensive approach to understanding the mindset of an inventor and the goals of their business. When he's not protecting great ideas, Chris enjoys hiking the many mountains of Southern California.

Made in the USA
Coppell, TX
27 September 2022

83689260R00049